God's Word

The Lutheran Difference Series

Michael Middendorf

with contributions by

Robert C. Baker

CONCORDIA PUBLISHING HOUSE • SAINT LOUIS

Written by Michael Middendorf

This publication may be available in braille, in large print, or on cassette tape for the visually impaired. Please allow 8 to 12 weeks for delivery. Write to the Library for the Blind, 7550 Watson Rd., St. Louis, MO 63119-4409; call 1-888-215-2455; or visit the Web site: www.blindmission.org.

Contents

About This Series

"Why doesn't your church really care about people?"

"What do you mean?"

"You won't allow committed gay couples to marry in your church."

"But . . . doesn't the Bible talk about adultery?"

"Sure it does. But today we know so much more about psychology than they did in Bible times. The Bible supports people loving each other. That's the main thing today."

As Lutherans interact with other Christians, they often find themselves struggling to explain their beliefs and practices. Although many Lutherans have learned the "what" of the doctrines of the church, they do not always have a full scriptural foundation to share the "why." When confronted with different doctrines, they cannot clearly state their faith, much less understand the differences.

Because of insecurities about explaining particular doctrines or practices, some Lutherans may avoid opportunities to share what they have learned from Christ and His Word. The Lutheran Difference Bible study series will identify how Lutherans differ from other Christians and show from the Bible why Lutherans differ. These studies will prepare Lutherans to share their faith and help non-Lutherans understand the Lutheran difference.

Student Introduction

"If there is only one Bible, why are there so many different denominations?"

"Why do churches agree on some points and disagree on others?"

"Which interpretation of this verse is correct?"

We rely on *assumptions* to interpret, or understand, any form of writing. The same is true for the Bible. We use *what we already believe* to help us understand God's Word.

For example, if we believe our God can and does accomplish miracles in the created world, we may accept the biblical stories of Jonah and Lazarus as historically true. However, if we believe God cannot or does not work this way, we may assume these accounts to be fictional stories created by authors trying to prove some spiritual point. If we hold that Jesus is both fully divine and fully human, we may accept His death on the cross as the sacrificial atonement for our sins. On the other hand, if we believe that Christ was simply a remarkable human being, we may suppose this teaching to have been developed by pious Christians in order to preserve the collective memory of the Master.

Lutherans maintain assumptions in interpreting the Holy Scriptures. In the Scriptures, Christ points to the truthfulness, reliability, and perfection of God's Word (Matthew 4:4; 5:17; Mark 12:24–27; Luke 4:21; 24:27, 44; John 5:39; 10:35; 17:17). Because the Holy Spirit gives faith in Christ as our Savior, and because He directs us to God's Word, Lutherans seek to interpret the Bible with humility, relying on the guidance and direction of the Holy Spirit as He leads us to Christ.

Lutheran assumptions in biblical interpretation can be summarized as follows:

- **God's Word, because it is His Word, is without error** (John 10:35; 17:17, 2 Timothy 3:16–17; 2 Peter 1:21). This means
  - the Bible cannot lie or deceive (Psalm 19:7; 119:7; John 10:35; 17:17; Romans 3:4; 2 Timothy 3:16–17; 2 Peter 1:21);
  - His Word is the only rule for faith and life (Psalm 119:105; 1 Corinthians 4:6; Galatians 1:6–9).
- **Christ is the heart and center of God's Word** (John 5:39; Acts 10:43). This means
  - the doctrine of justification by God's grace through faith in Christ is the chief doctrine of the Scriptures (John 3:16–17; Galatians 4:4–5; Hebrews 2:14–17; 1 Timothy 1:15);
  - Law and Gospel should be carefully distinguished (John 1:17; 2 Corinthians 3:6).
- **The Holy Spirit helps us to understand God's Word** (Psalm 119:73; John 14:26; 1 Corinthians 2:14). This means
  - difficult passages of Scripture are to be interpreted by other, clearer passages (Acts 17:11);
  - in humility we derive the plain meaning of words from their literal sense, unless clearly directed otherwise by context (2 Timothy 3:15).

Sometimes it is difficult to understand why, if everyone is using the same Bible, there are different teachings across denominational lines. The differences do not reside in the written text, that is, the shapes formed by ink on paper. Rather, they lie primarily in the *assumptions* made by the readers. How do these Lutheran assumptions of biblical interpretation compare or contrast with those of other church bodies? How do they compare to your own?

An Overview of Christian Denominations

The following outline of Christian history will help you understand where the different denominations come from and how they are related to one another. Use this outline in connection with the "Comparisons" sections found throughout the study. Statements of belief for the different churches are drawn from their official confessional writings.

The Great Schism

Eastern Orthodox: On July 16, 1054, Cardinal Humbert entered the Cathedral of the Holy Wisdom in Constantinople just before the worship service. He stepped to the altar and left a letter condemning Michael Cerularius, patriarch of Constantinople. Cerularius responded by condemning the letter and its authors. In that moment, Christian churches of the East and West were severed from each other. Their disagreements centered on what bread could be used in the Lord's Supper and the addition of the filioque statement to the Nicene Creed.

The Reformation

Lutheran: On June 15, 1520, Pope Leo X wrote a letter condemning Dr. Martin Luther for his Ninety-five Theses. Luther's theses had challenged the sale of indulgences, a fund-raising effort to pay for the building of St. Peter's Cathedral in Rome. The letter charged Luther with heresy and threatened to excommunicate him if he did not retract his writings within 60 days. Luther replied by publicly burning the letter. Leo excommunicated him on January 3, 1521, and condemned all who agreed with Luther or supported his cause.

Reformed: In 1522 the preaching of Ulrich Zwingli in Zurich, Switzerland, convinced people to break their traditional Lenten fast. Also, Zwingli preached that priests should be allowed to marry. When local friars challenged these departures from medieval church practice, the Zurich Council supported Zwingli and agreed that the Bible should guide Christian doctrine and practice. Churches of the Reformed tradition include Presbyterians and Episcopalians.

Anabaptist: In January 1525 Conrad Grebel, a follower of Ulrich Zwingli, rebaptized Georg Blaurock. Blaurock began rebaptizing others and founded the Swiss Brethren. Their insistence on adult believers' Baptism distinguished them from other churches of the Reformation. Anabaptists attracted social extremists who advocated violence in the cause of Christ, complete pacifism, or communal living. Mennonite, Brethren, and Amish churches descend from this movement.

The Counter Reformation

Roman Catholic: When people call the medieval church "Roman Catholic," they make a common historical mistake. Roman Catholicism as we know it emerged after the Reformation. As early as 1518 Luther and other reformers had appealed to the pope and requested a council to settle the issue of indulgences. Their requests were hindered or denied for a variety of theological and political reasons. Finally, on December 13, 1545, 34 leaders from the churches who opposed the Reformation gathered at the invitation of Pope Paul III. They began the Council of Trent (1545–63), which established the doctrine and practice of Roman Catholicism.

Post-Reformation Movements

Baptist: In 1608 or 1609 John Smyth, a former pastor of the Church of England, baptized himself by pouring water over his head. He formed a congregation of English Separatists in Holland, who opposed the rule of bishops and infant Baptism. This marked the start of the English Baptist churches, which remain divided doctrinally over the theology of John Calvin (Particular Baptists) and Jacob Arminius (General Baptists). In the 1800s the Restoration Movement of Alexander Campbell, a former Presbyterian minister, adopted many Baptist teachings. These churches include the Disciples of Christ (Christian Churches) and the Churches of Christ.

Wesleyan: In 1729 John and Charles Wesley gathered with three other men to study the Scripture, receive Communion, and discipline one another according to the "method" laid down in the Bible. Later, John Wesley's preaching caused religious revivals in England and America. Methodists, Wesleyans, Nazarenes, and Pentecostals form the Wesleyan family of churches.

Liberal: In 1799 Friedrich Schleiermacher published *Addresses on Religion* in an attempt to make Christianity appealing to people influenced by rationalism. He argued that religion is not a body of doctrines, provable truths, or a system of ethics, but belongs to the realm of feelings. His ideas did not lead to the formation of a new denomination, but deeply influenced Christian thinking. Denominations most thoroughly affected by liberalism are the United Church of Christ, Disciples of Christ, and Unitarianism.

Lutheran Facts

All who worship the Holy Trinity and trust in Jesus Christ for the forgiveness of sins are regarded by Lutherans as fellow Christians, despite denominational differences.

Lutheran churches first described themselves as *evangelische* or evangelical churches. Opponents of these churches called them *Lutheran* after Dr. Martin Luther, the sixteenth-century German church reformer.

Lutherans are not disciples of Dr. Martin Luther but disciples of Jesus Christ. They proudly accept the name Lutheran because they agree with Dr. Luther's teaching from the Bible, as summarized in Luther's Small Catechism.

Lutherans believe the Bible is God's inspired and inerrant (without error) Word. The Book of Concord refers to the "unchanging" and "infallible" truth of God's Word, which "cannot and will not deceive us." In his Large Catechism, Luther confesses, "God's Word cannot deceive." He urges us to "believe the Scriptures, which will not lie to you."

The Word of God permeates Lutheran worship services. The liturgy is full of direct quotations from Scripture. Hymns, if not quoting the Bible directly, paraphrase passages and themes. Sermons are based on specific texts of God's Word.

Lutherans also emphasize teaching God's Word to children and adults. Memorization of Bible passages is emphasized in Lutheran schools, Sunday schools, adult Bible studies, and at home.

Lutherans believe that God's Word exposes the deepest thoughts and desires of the human heart (Hebrews 4:12). At the same time, it powerfully gives new birth through the Gospel (1 Peter 1:23).

Because of this, Lutherans believe that God's Word of Gospel is a means of grace.

To prepare for "And God Said . . ." read 2 Timothy 3:16–17.

10

And God Said . . .

The ghost of Hamlet's father disappears at will and reappears only to have his son revenge his murder. Like the ghost, the gods of most religions seem interested in humanity only when it suits their own purposes. Selfish and self-serving, they enter and exit the stage of human history at their convenience.

Is there a God? How do we know? How can we know what God is like? How does God relate to people in general and to me specifically? Questions like these are at the heart of almost every religion, including Christianity. The answers to them also form the heart and basis of our lives.

1. We often hear, "Actions speak louder than words." What does this phrase mean? Do actions speak louder than words? Do you learn more about people from what they say or by what they do? Which do you tend to judge or evaluate people on more?

2. Look at your own words and actions. Do they always agree? If not, why not?

In the case of the God of the Scriptures, His words often speak louder than, or at least as loud as, His actions.

God Speaks

3. Read Romans 1:19–20 and Psalm 19:1–4. If God had not spoken to us, would we know there is a God? What can we know about God even apart from Him speaking to us?

4. Already in Genesis 1, God spoke. In fact, which happened first, God speaking or God acting? Read Genesis 1:1–3. Notice how this pattern continues through the rest of Genesis 1. Right from the beginning, what do these verses say about the nature of God and the speaking of God?

5. We communicate with others in a number of ways—by what we say and don't say and by what we do and don't do. It has been said, "It is better to keep your mouth closed and let people think you are a fool than to open it and remove all doubt." What is the point of that saying?

6. Just the opposite is true when God speaks! His words reveal more and more of His wisdom and goodness to us. In fact, it is only through God's Word in the Bible that we are able to know God personally and hear His plan of salvation. According to John 17:3, why is it important for us to know God in this way?

7. According to the Scriptures, God's existence, along with His power and majesty, are revealed in nature (natural revelation or natural knowledge of God). However, Christians acknowledge that God more

specifically reveals additional information about Himself to us in the Bible. What are some things God reveals about Himself in His Word? See, for example, Malachi 3:6; Leviticus 19:2; Exodus 20:5–6; Psalm 90:2.

8. Even though God has revealed Himself to us in the Scriptures, are there still some things about God that remain unknown to us? See Isaiah 55:8–9 and Romans 11:33–36. Is this good or bad, helpful or harmful to us?

9. Words are often necessary in order to explain actions. In the same way, actions can explain words. How do God's words and actions come together as one? Read 2 Corinthians 1:18–20 and 2 Corinthians 4:6. What or who is God's final and ultimate "word"? Explain. (Note: we will spend much more time on this in "The Word and the Word Made Flesh.")

Where Do We Look?

10. Stop and think about the ways many people are searching for God, for meaning in life, and for spiritual truth. Where do they look to find them? Where do you? What are your sources for knowledge about God? Is our human reason or experience a source for answers to these questions of ultimate importance?

11. The Bible is our only authoritative source for knowledge about God. There God speaks about Himself in His own words! It is significant that the phrase "The word of the LORD came" is used over 70 times in the Old Testament. It reveals that the God of the Scriptures first comes to us and speaks His Word to us. How does St. Paul make this same point in Romans 10:8–11, 14, and 17? What does Deuteronomy 8:3, as quoted by Jesus in Matthew 4:4, have to say about the purpose of God's Word and our search for a meaningful life?

The People's Voice

12. People often try to describe and characterize God or to say what God would or would not do. Listen during the week for such comments. Where do those assertions about God come from? How do you know what God is like or how He will act in your life? How can Christians respond when others assert things about God which are contradicted by His own words in the Bible?

13. Finally, in contrast with God's words, let's take a look at our own words. During this week, think about your words. What do they reveal to others about what you are like? Are your words and actions consistent? What does James 3:9–12 say about how we should and should not speak?

Comparisons

Eastern Orthodox: "The most ancient and original instrument for spreading divine revelation is holy tradition. From Adam to Moses there were no sacred books. Our Lord Jesus Christ Himself delivered His divine doctrine and ordinances to His

Disciples by word and example, but not by writing. The same method was followed by the Apostles also at first, when they spread abroad the faith and established the Church of Christ. The necessity of tradition is further evident from this, that books can be available only to a small part of mankind, but tradition to all." (*The Longer Catechism of the Eastern Church*, question 21).

Lutheran: "We believe, teach, and confess that the sole rule and standard according to which all dogmas together with teachers should be estimated and judged are the prophetic and apostolic Scriptures of the Old and of the New Testament alone, as it is written Psalm 119:105, 'Thy Word is a lamp unto my feet and a light unto my path.' And St. Paul: 'Though an angel from heaven preach any other gospel unto you, let him be accursed,' Galatians 1:8" (*Formula of Concord*, Epitome, article 1.1).

Presbyterian/Reformed: "Although the light of nature, and the works of creation and providence, do so far manifest the goodness, wisdom and power of God, as to leave men inexcusable; yet are they not sufficient to give that knowledge of God, and of His will, which is necessary unto salvation; therefore it pleased the Lord, at sundry times, and in divers manners, to reveal Himself, and to declare that His will unto His Church; and afterwards, for the better preserving and propagating of the truth, and for the more sure establishment and comfort of the Church against the corruption of the flesh, and the malice of Satan and of the world, to commit the same wholly unto writing; which maketh the holy Scripture to be most necessary; those former ways of God's revealing His will unto His people being now ceased" (*Westminster Confession of Faith*, ch. 1).

Roman Catholic: "The sacred and holy, oecumenical and general Synod of Trent—lawfully assembled in the Holy Ghost, the same Legates of the Apostolic See presiding therein . . . receives and venerates with an equal affection of piety, and reverence, all the books both of the Old and of the New Testament—seeing that one God is the author of both—as also the said traditions . . . preserved in the Catholic Church by a continuous succession" (*Canons and Decrees of the Council of Trent*, Session 24, Decree Concerning the Canonical Scriptures).

Baptist: "We believe that the Holy Bible was written by men divinely inspired, and is a perfect treasure of heavenly instruction; that it has God for its author, salvation for its end, and truth without any mixture of error for its matter; that it reveals the principles by which God will judge us; and therefore is, and shall remain to the end of the world, the true center of Christian union, and the supreme standard by which all human conduct, creeds, and opinions should be tried" (*New Hampshire Baptist Confession*, article 1).

Methodist/Wesleyan: "The Holy Scriptures contain all things necessary to salvation; so that whatsoever is not read therein, nor may be proved thereby, is not to be required of any man that it should be believed as an article of faith, or be thought requisite or necessary to salvation." (*Methodist Articles of Religion*, article 5).

Liberal Protestant: "The facts of history have shown that Paul was in error in his teaching in 1 Thessalonians about the coming of the Lord in the clouds of heaven. It is a palpable infidelity to truth to affirm that this teaching was true; it is a double error to transfer it to the present time and reaffirm it for our own day. Some portions of his teachings about marriage and spiritual gifts, however adapted to meet the needs of the Corinthians, are impossible of reaffirmation today. Whether the preacher in the pulpit passes these things over in silence and limits himself to the things that have attested themselves as true by the test of human experience, as may often be his wisest course or the teacher finds it necessary to deal with them explicitly, honestly, and frankly, as he must if they come up for consideration at all, both the preaching and the teaching will be made more effective religiously and morally than when it is assumed that all the views of the New Testament writers are equally valuable" (Ernest DeWitt Burton in *A Guide to the Study of the Christian Religion*, Gerald Birney Smith, ed., pp. 236–37).

Point to Remember

In the past God spoke to our forefathers through the prophets at many times and in various ways, but in these last days He has spoken to us by His Son. Hebrews 1:1–2

To prepare for "Now That's Inspired!" read 2 Peter 1:21.

Now That's Inspired!

"Welcome to Port Royal, Mr. Smith."

—Harbormaster in the film *Pirates of the Caribbean: The Curse of the Black Pearl*

The harbormaster in the seaside town of Port Royal was inspired. Captain Jack Sparrow, eccentric seaman and rogue pirate, had made two requests: docking space for his "ship" and the harbormaster's "amnesia" when it came to last names. The harbormaster granted Sparrow's requests, but his inspiration to help came at a price: three shillings tossed on his open ledger.

Money may inspire some people to bend the rules. For others, inspiration toward action must come from another source. The promise of better benefits or shorter working hours may motivate someone to change jobs. The desire for a better appearance may encourage a dieter to remain faithful to the diet plan. Thoughts of sunny, windswept beaches may compel a family to save a few extra dollars each week for that much-needed vacation.

14. Someone may leave a concert, a lecture, a movie, or even a worship service and say, "That was truly inspiring!" After looking at a beautiful sunset or mountain, one could respond, "That really inspires me!" What do we mean by those uses of the word *inspire*?

15. What do you think is meant when people speak of God's Word with terms like *inspired* and *inspiration*? The church's doctrine of inspiration tries to answer the question "Is the Bible man's words or God's Word?" What do you think? Mark the following true or false:

a. _____ God dictated His Word. Each author's own personality was *not* involved.

b. _____ God worked through the abilities, personality, background, and training of various authors to speak His Word to people.

17

c. _____ The words written in the Bible *are* the "words" of God.

d. _____ God gave the authors *thoughts*; the authors put them in their own words.

e. _____ The Bible merely *contains* the Word of God. Some words are God's; some are simply human.

f. _____ God revealed the *basic Gospel* message to the authors of Scripture. When they address other topics, they are giving their own thoughts/opinions.

g. _____ The words in the Bible are basically human words, containing the personal biases and prejudices of the authors.

h. _____ The Bible contains God's Word to the people and churches of *those days*. They do not apply in the same way today.

i. _____ The Bible is God's words to the churches of *today,* and they should all be applied literally.

j. _____ The Bible gives specific directions from God to His people in the days they originally addressed. The teachings/doctrines/ principles still apply, but the applications in our day may differ.

So is the Bible the words of man and/or God's Word? Ultimately, the church has concluded that the answer is "both/and." Logically, it may be impossible for words to be both from men and from God. As a result, the church has concluded this is a "mystery" and a miracle of God which cannot be completely explained to our human reason. But to talk about this issue, theologians typically use the term *inspiration.*

Divine Author/Human Authors

16. Read 2 Timothy 3:14–17. What, specifically, was St. Paul referring to in his day by the phrase "all Scripture" (v. 16)? What does he say about Scripture in the first half of verse 16? What does this mean?

17. Read 2 Peter 1:20–21. What is Peter talking about with the phrase "prophecy of Scripture"? What does he say about the authorship of Scripture? What ways of describing how the Scriptures came into being does this exclude as improper?

18

18. "Thus says the LORD." The Old Testament prophets use that phrase or something very similar over 350 times! Why is this significant?

19. How did this process of inspiration work with specific Old Testament prophets and prophecy? See, for example, the prophet Jeremiah in 1:9; 26:2; 20:9; and 15:16. Compare Ezekiel 2:9–3:4 and Isaiah 6:1–9.

20. In light of your answers to questions 16 and 17, what else can be included as God-inspired Scripture according to the following passages?

a. John 6:63

b. 1 Corinthians 11:23 and 15:3

c. Galatians 1:1–2, 11–12

d. 1 Thessalonians 2:13

e. 1 Corinthians 14:36–38

f. 1 Timothy 5:18

g. 2 Peter 3:15–16

21. According to John 14:25–26 and 16:12–15, what role did the Holy Spirit play in bringing the Word of Jesus to us through the New Testament apostles?

A Great and Holy Helper

22. What clear distinction does St. Paul make about the ability of people to understand God's Word in 1 Corinthians 2:11–16? How can we understand what God is speaking in His Word based on this passage (see also Luke 24:45)?

23. According to the passage read in question 21, we need the Spirit before we can understand the Word of God. Yet Jesus says His words are "Spirit and are life" (John 6:63). So which comes first to us, the Word or the Spirit? Is this like "Which came first, the chicken or the egg?"

Every Good Work

24. According to the 2 Timothy passage read above (3:14–17), what is the main purpose of Scripture in your life? What are some other roles which Scripture is to perform? How does it do this?

25. Can you and/or others be inspired by God today and during this week? Look and listen for "inspired" words from God.

Comparisons

Verbal Inspiration: The Holy Spirit led the prophets, evangelists, and apostles to write the books of the Bible. He guided their writing, inspiring their very words, while working through their particular styles of expression. Therefore, the Bible's words are God's Word. Conservative Christian churches hold this view. Many also maintain that the original writings of the Bible were without error (inerrancy) but that some mistakes entered the text as the scribes copied, edited, or translated the Scriptures over the centuries.

Partial Inspiration: Christians affected by theological liberalism hold different views of the inspiration of the Bible. For example, some would assert that the Bible is God's Word but that the authors erred in some factual details. Others would say that the Bible contains God's Word and that the Spirit leads people today to determine which parts of the Bible God wants them to follow. Still others would say that the Bible is one testimony to God's Word, along with writings used in other religions.

Inspired Translations: Some churches hold that God inspired certain translations of the Bible. For example, the Eastern Orthodox Church holds that the Greek Septuagint translation of the Old Testament was inspired by God. Some English-speaking Protestants hold that God inspired the King James translation of the Bible.

Point to Remember

The Counselor, the Holy Spirit, whom the Father will send in My name, will teach you all things and will remind you of everything I have said to you. John 14:26

To prepare for "God's Pen Is Mightier than All!" read Isaiah 55:10–11 and John 10:35.

God's Pen Is Mightier Than All!

"Every man will read a book with more pleasure or even with more ease, if it is written in fairer characters."

—Epictetus, *Discourses*

The early second-century Stoic philosopher Epictetus believed that happiness was attainable only by living virtuously and taming one's passions. His *Discourses,* possibly penned by Arrius, his disciple, extol the power of the human soul and the authority of human reason. Affected by ill health and misfortune throughout most of his life, Epictetus nevertheless sought well-being from within.

Epictetus's pen has played a formative role in the study of philosophy. For some, his writings have encouraged self-denial and close introspection in order to obtain contentment. But do Epictetus's words continue to have the power and authority they once did? Or have they, like the works of so many other philosophers, been relegated to the dusty shelves of history?

26. "The pen is mightier than the sword." What does that phrase mean? What are some times in history when it has proven true?

27. God's Word was probably originally written with a sharpened piece of reed or, perhaps, some type of quill. But we can say God "penned" His Word to us through various authors. So which is mightier, the penned Word of God or the sword? What does Ephesians 6:17 have to say about this? Why does Paul compare the Word of God to a sword?

Power and Authority

28. Read Isaiah 55:10–11. What is the comparison with the Word of the Lord? What points do these verses make about the Lord's Word?

29. In our first lesson, Genesis 1 revealed the power and authority of God's Word. Explain.

30. God's powerful Word is compared to what in Jeremiah 23:29?

31. An analogy similar to Isaiah 55 is used by Jesus in the parable of the sower. What is God's Word like according to Luke 8:5–15? See especially verse 11. What is the power of the Word compared to in this parable?

32. Hebrews 4:12 speaks of the Word of God as a _____. What five very descriptive "points" does the author of Hebrews make about God's Word?

33. The power of God's Word is proclaimed in both Law and Gospel. What does Jesus say will judge the world in John 12:48? According to Romans 1:16–17, what is the ultimate power of God?

Seed That Lasts

34. Read 1 Peter 1:23–2:3. This passage says a number of things that relate the Word of God to our own lives. What is Peter trying to say about life apart from God's Word when he quotes Isaiah in verses 24–25? How is God's Word different?

35. Phrases like "born again" (1:23) and "newborn babies" make us think about what part of the Christian life? How does this relate to God's Word? See "The Nature of Baptism" and "The Power of Baptism" in Martin Luther's Small Catechism (*Lutheran Worship,* p. 303).

36. In the original Greek language, verse 2 calls us to desire the "pure spiritual milk of God's Word." Why do we "crave" it? What does it seek to accomplish in our lives?

Well-Armed

37. One of St. Paul's analogies for the Christian life is to describe us as soldiers of the cross in Ephesians 6:10–17. Read those verses.

What are the opponents aligned against the believer? Note that the items he mentions are all defensive armor, except for perhaps two of them. What are the pieces of defensive armor in your life? Where do they come from? What is your main offensive weapon, described here as "the sword of the Spirit"?

38. As Christians go out on the offensive, this weapon may sometimes be offensive to others! Remember the passage from Hebrews above? (4:12; question 32). How is the Word of God offensive in our day in terms of both Law and Gospel? Look for ways to go out on the offensive with God's Word during this week. As Christian soldiers go onward, with what, according to the end of verse 15, are they also equipped?

Comparisons

Eastern Orthodox: "We undoubtingly confess, as sure truth, that the Catholic Church cannot sin, nor err, nor utter falsehood in place of truth; for the Holy Ghost, ever working through His faithful ministers the fathers and doctors of the Church, preserves her from all error" (Missive of the Eastern Patriarchs on the Orthodox Faith, Art. 12, quoted in *The Longer Catechism of the Eastern Church*, answer 271).

Lutheran: "In this way the distinction between the Holy Scriptures of the Old and of the New Testament and all other writings is preserved, and the Holy Scriptures alone remain the only judge, rule, and standard, according to which as the only test-stone, all dogmas shall and must be discerned and judged, as to whether they are good or evil, right or wrong" (*Formula of Concord*, Epitome, article 1.7).

Presbyterian/Reformed: "We may be moved and induced by the testimony of the Church to a high and reverent esteem of the holy

Scripture; and the heavenliness of the matter, the efficacy of the doctrine, the majesty of the style, the consent of all the parts, the scope of the whole (which is to give all glory to God), the full discovery it makes of the only way of man's salvation, the many other incomparable excellencies, and the entire perfection thereof, are arguments whereby it doth abundantly evidence itself to be the Word of God; yet, notwithstanding, our full persuasion and assurance of the infallible truth, and divine authority thereof, is from the inward Word of the Holy Spirit, bearing witness by and with the Word in our hearts" (*Westminster Confession of Faith*, chapter 1, V).

Roman Catholic: "The Roman Pontiff, when he speaks *ex cathedra* . . . is possessed of that infallibility with which the divine Redeemer wills that His Church should be endowed for defining doctrine regarding faith or morals" (First Vatican Council, *Pastor aeternus,* ch. 4, July 18, 1870).

Conservative Protestants: Generally agree that the Holy Scriptures are authoritative in all areas of faith and life, and derive their doctrine and practice from their respective understandings of the Bible.

Liberal Protestants: Vary in submission to the authority of God's Word depending on their beliefs about its accuracy and inspiration. Viewpoints may range from seeing the Bible as a mere historical book irrelevant to modern theology and morality to regarding only the teachings about Christ as inspired and authentic.

Point to Remember

Beginning with Moses and all the Prophets, He explained to them what was said in all the Scriptures concerning Himself. Luke 24:27

To prepare for "You Have My Word on It!" read Acts 17:11.

You Have My Word on It!

"We will not vanish without a fight. We're going to live on. We're going to survive."

—President Thomas J. Whitmore in the film *Independence Day*

With the future of humanity hanging in the balance, Thomas J. Whitmore had a job to do. The heroics of flying his jet and firing on the alien hordes would come later. First, he must address his squadron, which was discouraged by the tactical and technological power of the enemy. With loudspeaker in hand, he opened his mouth. And the squadron held on to his every word.

How many times have you heard or said the words of our title? What are some times when you have been given someone else's "word on it" and their word proved to be untrue? How did this change your image of that person? How do you feel about yourself when you are unable to keep your word?

Here is a brief, historical overview to set the stage for today's lesson. History progressed through the Middle/Dark Ages into the Renaissance, which heralded a "rebirth" of learning. The Renaissance occurred around the time of the Reformation (1500s). This was followed by the Age of Rationalism, or the Enlightenment, a period governed by the supremacy of human reason and the modern, scientific method. The human mind, it was asserted, could solve all problems and was the ultimate authority.

However, rationalism underwent many challenges during the twentieth century in science, politics, and religion. Scholars often speak of our culture today with the term *postmodernism*. Postmodernism tends to reject any absolute truth. It also attempts to allow competing or apparently contradictory truths to "peacefully" coexist in the areas of science, politics, and, even or especially, religion. One could say that the theories of relativity have not only impacted the world of physics. They have also reached into the fields of morality (e.g., situational ethics), politics (e.g., "spin" or "might makes right"), and religion (e.g., New Age).

27

39. What evidence do you see of this in your world?

Jesus says to the Father, "Your word is truth" (John 17:17). Those words and this lesson are a particular challenge for those in a postmodern culture to accept.

One Book, Many Books

Christians speak of the Bible as God's Word of truth. However, we often view the Bible as if it were one book. Actually, the Bible is a collection or library of 66 different documents written over a period of more than 1,000 years by at least 30 different human authors! How did these documents "become" the Bible? The technical term for this issue is "the canon." *Canon* is a Greek word for a "reed" or "straight rod." It came to be used like we use the term "a measuring stick." As a result, when the word *canon* is used of the Holy Scriptures, it expresses that these documents are the authoritative "measuring stick" for what we believe about God, the world, and ourselves.

Who decided that the 66 books in the canon were the divinely revealed "Truth" of God? The Old Testament books were regarded as authoritative as soon as they were given through Moses and the other authors. As a result, in practical use and understanding, an Old Testament canon existed throughout the history of Israel, beginning with Moses. However, the specific 39 books in our Old Testament were not identified as such until around the time of Christ. In regard to the 27 documents we speak of as the New Testament, the situation was quite similar. The early church immediately used the words of Jesus and Paul and regarded them as authoritative (see point 21 in "Now That's Inspired!"). However, it was not until the late fourth century that the 27 documents in the Bible were specifically listed as the New Testament canon.

It may seem troublesome at first to acknowledge that God never gave a specific list for the Old or New Testament; neither is the formation of the canon a scientifically verifiable process. Rather, in regard to establishing both the Old and New Testament collections, the circumstances were similar. There was an ongoing, nearly unanimous

28

acceptance of most of the books as the divinely inspired Word of God. A few books that were questioned by some (e.g., Esther, Daniel, Revelation) gradually came to be included and then universally recognized by the church. At the same time, books about which there was dispute and uncertainty (e.g., Ecclesiasticus, the Shepherd of Hermes) were excluded. Ultimately, the acceptance of these 66 documents as the Bible is a matter of faith in the God who gave them, who preserved them for us, who handed them down to us, and who continues to speak His Word of truth through them today.

40. What do these verses say about the truth of God's Word?
a. Psalm 12:6

b. Psalm 119:86, 89, 138, 151, 160

c. 2 Samuel 22:31

d. John 10:35

e. John 17:17

41. In light of your previous responses, think about the prophet Jonah. He was sent by the Lord to announce that in 40 days Nineveh would be destroyed (3:3–4). However, that did not happen (3:10). Was Jonah's prophecy, and therefore God's Word, untrue? How can you reconcile this and still maintain the truthfulness of Scripture? See Jeremiah 18:7–10 and James 2:13.

42. If God's Word is truth, how does this relate to what Jesus says about Himself in John 14:6? This will lead us into the next and final lesson.

True to the Text

43. What is the purpose or role of God's truthful Word in our lives according to John 17:17? How does this fit into God's Word being truth? What does this reveal about the nature and purpose of God speaking to us? Compare this with God's relationship to His Old Testament people based upon Leviticus 20:8 (see Leviticus 11:45).

44. If God's Word is held up as the truth for God's people, what must God's people guard against according to the last sentence of Matthew 15:6? What are some examples where this has been a problem in the history of the church? What about today?

Certain Truth

45. In what areas of life today is the truth of God's Word openly and often challenged? How should a Christian respond?

46. Jesus says to the Father, "Your word is truth" (John 17:17). What is the difference between God's Word being true and God's

Word being truth? In our day of competing truths or even a rejection of the existence of absolute truth in any form, what do the Scriptures say?

Comparisons

Many philosophical ideas in our society compete for our attention and acceptance. In addition to rationalism and postmodernism (discussed earlier this chapter), other "-isms" jockey for position when we study the absolute and changeless truths of the Bible. Often Bible readers are not even aware that such ideas influence and color their interpretation of God's Word.

Rationalism: "We can figure that out." Rejects religious faith or dogma in determining truth, and relies solely on human reason and analysis. Secular humanism, which deifies the human person, human society and its achievements, and atheism, which denies that God exists, are philosophically related to rationalism.

Relativism: "Everything is relative." There is no absolute reference for the values human beings place in their beliefs or behaviors. As a philosophical theory, relativism has two inherent problems: either it is itself relativistic (that is, subject to change) or absolutist (by claiming there are no absolutes).

Moral Relativism: "There are no moral absolutes." Morals arise from society's agreed-upon customs, traditions, or etiquette. In contrast, moral absolutists believe that timeless norms are not culture-bound but are derived from natural law, human nature, religious sources, or a combination of these.

Subjectivism: "Perception creates reality." There is no true reality apart from our perception. Objectivists, however, argue that there is an underlying reality to all things existing independently of our perception. Subjectivism tends also to conflict with everyday human experience.

Pragmatism: "Whatever works is right." This notably American philosophical system sets goals as standards of reality, and judges concepts by how well they help achieve those goals. Although in many cases quite helpful, pragmatism's chief weaknesses lie in determining the inherent value of the desired goals and deciding who or what makes those determinations.

Point to Remember

I admit that I worship the God of our fathers as a follower of the Way, which they call a sect. I believe everything that agrees with the Law and that is written in the Prophets. Acts 24:14

To prepare for "The Word and the Word Made Flesh," read John 5:39 and Acts 10:43.

The Word and the Word Made Flesh

"Lord, keep us steadfast in your Word;
Curb those who by deceit or sword
Would wrest the kingdom from your Son
And bring to nought all he has done."

—Martin Luther, *Lutheran Worship* 334

To Martin Luther the primary focus of the Scriptures was God's grace, mercy, and forgiveness through Jesus Christ. The Bible served as a sort of manger, Luther said, in which the Christ Child was laid. Throughout his often tumultuous life, Luther would go to that manger to encounter his Savior. There a little child could give him something the grown-up world could not: comfort and hope in the midst of every trouble.

We began this study with the phrase "Actions speak louder than words." Fortunately, with God there is no dichotomy between the two. God speaks and it happens. God promises and He fulfills. But there is even more here. The Scriptures teach that God's Word became a person in Jesus of Nazareth. Scripture speaks of this as the doctrine of the incarnation, from the Latin word meaning "in-fleshed." This is the focus of our final study of the Word of God.

Getting to the Point

47. Jesus says some very interesting things about the Scriptures, the written Word of God. What does Jesus say in the following passages about the focal point of the Old Testament Scriptures?

a. John 5:39–40

b. John 5:46–47

c. Luke 24:44–47

48. Other passages in the New Testament make a similar point about Jesus. What is said about the relationship between Jesus and the Old Testament Scriptures in Hebrews 1:1 and in 1 Peter 1:10–12?

49. Jesus not only states that the Scriptures spoke about Him. He also announces what about His own words in John 6:63? What does Peter say about Jesus' words in John 6:68?

50. However, the relationship between Jesus and the Word of God is even more full. Let us return again to the beginning in Genesis 1. How did God create all that exists (e.g. Genesis 1:3)?

51. John's Gospel also begins "in the beginning" (1:1). Read John 1:1–3. What does John identify as being present and active then? What remarkable statement does John make about the Word of God in John 1:14? See also Matthew 1:20–21 and Luke 1:35.

52. 1 John 1:1–4 also starts with what was "from the beginning." What does John mean when he states that he and others could hear, see, look at, and touch "the Word of life"? As he continues, what was the purpose of the incarnation or the Word "becoming flesh"?

53. Finally, in Revelation 19 John sees an individual on a white horse. How is this rider described in verses 11–16? What is the rider's name?

Finding the Center

54. According to the number of words in the King James Version of the Bible, 76 percent of God's words to us are in what we call the Old Testament. What impact does this statistic have on you? Remember 2 Timothy 3:16–17.

55. If Jesus is the center of the Scriptures, what does this mean for how we read, interpret, understand, and apply the Old Testament Word of God?

56. As we look toward the end of the world, what does Jesus say about our response to those awesome and sometimes frightening events in Luke 21:27–28 and 32–33?

Growing in the Gift

57. In "God's Pen Is Mightier Than All!" we read 1 Peter 1:23–2:2. 1 Peter 2:2–3 states, "Like newborn babes, crave pure spiritual milk, so that by it you may grow up in your salvation, now that you

have tasted that the Lord is good." Salvation is a gift, yet it is also something we can "grow up in" according to Peter. How is this true?

58. An end of study resolution: How can you personally resolve to grow up in your salvation by continuing to crave the pure, spiritual milk of God's Word?

Comparisons

Eastern Orthodox: *"Why, then, was holy Scripture given?* To this end, that divine revelation might be preserved more exactly and unchangeably" (*The Longer Catechism of the Eastern Church*, question 22).

Lutheran: "Therefore God, out of His immense goodness and mercy, has His divine eternal Law and His wonderful plan concerning our redemption, namely, the holy, alone-saving Gospel of His eternal Son, our only Savior and Redeemer, Jesus Christ, publicly preached; and by this collects an eternal Church for Himself from the human race, and works in the hearts of men true repentance and knowledge of sins, and true faith in the Son of God, Jesus Christ. And by this means, and in no other way, namely, through His holy Word, when men hear it preached or read it, and the holy Sacraments when they are used according to His Word, God desires to call men to eternal salvation, draw them to Himself, and convert, regenerate, and sanctify them" (*Formula of Concord*, Solid Declaration, article II, 50).

Presbyterian/Reformed: "The whole counsel of God, concerning all things necessary for His own glory, man's salvation, faith, and life, is either expressly set down in Scripture, or by good and necessary consequence may be deduced from Scripture: unto which nothing at any time is to be added, whether by new revelations of the Spirit, or traditions of men. Nevertheless we acknowledge the inward illumination of the Spirit of God to be necessary for the saving understanding of such things as are revealed in the Word." (*Westminster Confession of Faith*, ch. 1,

VI).

Roman Catholic: "Furthermore, in order to restrain petulant spirits, it [this Council] decrees, that no one, relying on his own skill, shall—in matters of faith, and of morals pertaining to the edification of Christian doctrine—wresting the sacred Scripture to his own senses, presume to interpret the said sacred Scripture contrary to that sense which holy mother Church—whose it is to judge of the true sense and interpretation of the Holy Scripture—hath held and doth hold" (*Canons and Decrees of the Council of Trent*, Session 24, Decree Concerning the Canonical Scriptures).

Baptist: "We believe that, in order to be saved, sinners must be regenerated, or born again; that regeneration consists in giving a holy disposition to the mind; that it is effected in a manner above our comprehension by the power of the Holy Spirit, in connection with divine truth, so as to secure our voluntary obedience to the Gospel; and that its proper evidence appears in the holy fruits of repentance, and faith, and newness of life" (*New Hampshire Baptist Confession*, article 7).

Methodist/Wesleyan: "The Holy Scriptures contain all things necessary to salvation; so that whatsoever is not read therein, nor may be proved thereby, is not to be required of any man that it should be believed as an article of faith, or be thought requisite or necessary to salvation." (*Methodist Articles of Religion*, article 5).

Liberal Protestant: "If the source of our sin is located in a non-psychological 'nature' which we inherit, we shall, of course, interpret the work of Christ in terms of His 'natures,' divine and human. But if we think of sin concretely and refer it to its psychological causes, we shall interpret salvation in terms of conscious experience. We shall then not ask concerning the 'nature' of Jesus, but rather concerning His religious consciousness and life. We shall emphasize His *God-consciousness* and His ability to create in His disciples a trust in God which gives spiritual insight and moral power" (*A Guide to the Study of the Christian Religion,* pp. 531–32).

Point to Remember

From infancy you have known the holy Scriptures, which are able to make you wise for salvation through faith in Jesus Christ. 2 Timothy 3:15

Leader Guide

This guide is provided as a "safety net," a place to turn for help in answering questions and enriching discussion. It will not answer every question raised in your class. Please read it, along with the questions, before class. Consult it in class only after exploring the Bible references and discussing what they teach. Please note the different abilities of your class members. Some will easily find the Bible passages listed in this study; others will struggle. To make participation easier, team up members of the class. For example, if a question asks you to look up several passages, assign one passage to one group, the second to another, and so on. Divide the work! Let participants present the answers they discover.

Each topic is divided into four easy-to-use sections.

Focus introduces key concepts that will be discovered.

Inform guides the participants into Scripture to uncover truths concerning a doctrine.

Connect enables participants to apply what is learned in Scripture to their lives and provides them an opportunity to formulate and articulate a defense of a key doctrine.

Vision provides participants with practical suggestions for extending the theme of the lesson out of the classroom and into the world.

Also take note of the Comparisons section at the end of each lesson. The editor has drawn this material from the official confessional documents and historical works of the various denominations. The passages describe and compare the denominations so that students can see how Lutherans differ from other Christians and also see how all Christians share many of the same beliefs and practices. The passages are not polemical.

And God Said . . .

Objectives

By the power of the Holy Spirit working through God's Word, participants will understand that (1) God's existence, as well as His power and majesty, are revealed in nature, yet we only know Him personally as He has spoken to us, (2) God has communicated Himself to us in His Word, the Holy Bible, and continues to speak to us today through those same Holy Scriptures, and (3) we know the most important truth, the Gospel/Good News of God, only through His Word.

Opening Worship

Sing "Thy Strong Word" (*LW* 328).

(Author's suggestions: You may sing the hymn or simply read through the stanzas. Stanzas 1–4 may be used at the opening; the last two stanzas serve as a good conclusion to this lesson. Note how the hymn takes us back to God speaking at creation [stanza 1]. However, it also points to how God's strong Word declares us righteous [stanza 3] and to the cross, the ultimate spoken "word" from God [stanza 4]. Stanza 5 is a response of sanctified living and speaking by us. The final stanza is a fitting doxology of praise. Another option is "And God Said, Yes!" by Terry Dittmer. You can find it in CPH's *Singing Saints Songbook*. It is based on the 2 Corinthians 1 passage used in the Inform section and nicely ties that text to Baptism.)

Focus

1. Have someone read the second paragraph. Ask for replies. Questions about "knowing God" will be brought up again in the Inform section. Read aloud the rest of the Focus section. Discuss the differences between speaking and action among humans.

39

2. Point out how we don't always say what we do or do what we say. This could be a good time for Law applications, but these are also brought out later in the Vision section, which uses James 3.

God Speaks (Inform)

(Author's note to leader: You may want to print out all the Bible passages in each of these lessons. Another option is to write out the references on separate slips of paper and give one or more to each participant. They can then look up their passages and use the paper as a bookmark. This will speed up and organize the study in case participants are unable to quickly find passages of Scripture.)

3. Romans 1 states that God's existence, eternal power, and divine nature are clearly seen in the creation around us. Psalm 19 asserts that the heavens and skies declare God's glory. Both passages emphasize how these are made plain to *all*.

4. In Genesis 1 "God said" first on each day of creation, and then things actually came into being. This reveals that God is a God who speaks words and that His words powerfully accomplish what He says.

5. When we speak we reveal our inadequacies and our inconsistencies. Sometimes these may remain hidden if we remain silent. The point here is that the very act of speaking is an act of self-revelation!

6. In this verse Jesus says what our salvation is based upon and how we come to have eternal life. These are ours only by knowing (being in relationship with) the true God and His Son, Jesus Christ.

7. This recaps question 3, but moves forward to what theologians call the "specific revelation" of God in the Scriptures. In Malachi 3 God reveals His unchanging nature. Leviticus 19 asserts His holiness. Exodus 20:5 is harsh Law. God declares that He is a jealous God. This is difficult since jealousy is normally understood as a sin. You may explain this with the term *zealous* and illustrate the concept in the marriage context. God's relationship with Israel at Mt. Sinai is something like a wedding ceremony uniting God and His people. God desires Israel for Himself and does not want to "share her" with other gods (vv. 4–5). However, point out that God's "mercy triumphs over judgment" (James 2:13) in verse 6. His love (Gospel) extends far beyond the bounds of His punishment (Law). In Psalm 90:2 God's eternal or everlasting nature is stated.

8. The doctrine of the "sufficiency of Scripture" asserts that God has revealed all that we need to know for our salvation, not that God reveals everything to us. Even for those of us who have the Scriptures, some of God's ways and thoughts are far beyond our present comprehension (Isaiah 55). God's wisdom, knowledge, judgments, and paths are more than we can fathom (Romans 11). These are reasons to have awe and respect for God and to praise Him for His glory.

9. In 2 Corinthians 1 Paul is specifically speaking about his travel plans for visiting the Corinthians. In that context, he makes a profound theological statement. God's promises were spoken by him. "As surely as God is faithful" (v. 18), they are all fulfilled or answered, "Yes!" and they are done so in Jesus Christ. Jesus was brought to the Corinthians through the proclamation of Paul, Silas and Timothy. In response, they are called to say "Amen" to the glory of God (v. 20). All of us have heard the same affirmative Word. All God's promises have been fulfilled for us in Christ, and we are called to give the same response. 2 Corinthians 4:6 goes back to God speaking at creation. God's speaking is fulfilled when His Word shines the light of Jesus Christ into our hearts.

Where Do We Look (Connect)

10. Similar questions were introduced at the beginning of the lesson. Here you may want to spend some time discussing them. Point out that rather than us looking for and finding God, God has come near and spoken to us. He speaks to us in His Word, the Bible, the Holy Scriptures. The Old Testament prophets use the phrase "The word of the LORD came" over 70 times to point out that God's Word came to them, not vice versa. In Romans 10 Paul quotes Deuteronomy 30;14 to assert that this was also true for the Israelites who were about to enter the Promised Land. God had spoken to them in His Word through Moses. Finally, He has come to reveal Himself in the person of Jesus Christ (Hebrews 1:1–2). Paul states that people cannot believe or be saved unless they hear the message "through the word of Christ" (v. 17). When "the word of faith" is proclaimed, God still draws near to people in order to save them through the message of Christ's death and resurrection. Our reason or experience cannot answer such important questions.

11. In Romans 10 Paul clearly states that God continues speaking to His people through the oral proclamation of His Word. In Matthew 4:4 Jesus is refuting the devil's temptation to turn stones into bread. Jesus quotes Deuteronomy 8:3 to declare that bread alone (earthly things, material possessions) does not give lasting life. Rather, God again comes to us in His Word and gives us life. We live on His Word and in His Word as well.

The People's Voice (Vision)

12. People in our day often accept a loving God who welcomes all. Many have concluded there is no hell and that God is love and would never send anybody there anyway. As a result, people do not usually think of God as a judge or view Jesus as having wrath (e.g. Revelation 6:16–17). On the other hand, the "particularity of the Gospel" is also a scandal to many (see especially John 14:6; Acts 4:12) who accept any and all religions as valid approaches to God. The Bible is the only authoritative source of our knowledge about God. The best way to respond to unbiblical statements about God is gently with a Bible in hand or by reciting specific Scripture passages. God's own words carry more "authority" with people than simply trying to summarize the Bible's or the church's teaching. This means we must know the Scriptures well to engage in such discussions.

13. Note that this is, in one sense, condemning Law. James begins chapter 3 by pointing out that "we all stumble in many ways" (v. 2). He proceeds to use various analogies to illustrate how we are unable to tame our tongue or to control the damage it causes (vv. 3–9). On the other hand, this is good third use of the Law. After hearing the gracious words of God spoken to us (points 6, 9, and 10 above), how should we speak in response? The words of verses 5 and 6 of "Thy Strong Word" are a fitting response. We praise God with our lips and use our mouths to speak to others about His mercy.

Now That's Inspired!

Objectives

By the power of the Holy Spirit working through God's Word, participants will (1) better understand the Scripture passages which serve as the basis for the doctrine of inspiration, (2) learn how the process of divine inspiration produced the Word of God in the Old and New Testaments, (3) comprehend the role of the Holy Spirit in this miraculous process, and (4) have some understanding of what inspiration does not mean.

(Author's note to leader: Scholars have distinguished God's *revelation* from His *inspiration* of the Scriptures. Revelation involves God revealing himself to people in previously unknown and unknowable ways. An example would be the burning bush [Exodus 3] and even the person of Jesus Christ. Inspiration is when God's truth is written down as Scripture, the content of which may or may not involve divine revelation as defined above. An example of inspiration without the need for divine revelation would be Luke recording the stops of Paul's missionary journeys in Acts. This may be too fine a distinction to bring up in the lesson.)

Opening Worship

Sing "God Has Spoken by His Prophets" (*LW* 343). If the tune is unfamiliar, you may speak the words or use a more familiar tune such as Galilean ("Hark, the Voice of Jesus Crying," *LW* 318). The verses do an excellent job of laying out how God spoke in the prophets (stanza 1) and, ultimately, in Jesus Christ (stanza 2). However, God continues to speak His inspired Word to us today as His Spirit works through the words of the Scriptures (stanza 3)!

Focus

14. Ask participants to define "inspire." You may want to bring a dictionary. See if people can distinguish common uses of the word "inspire" (e.g., to animate, arouse, affect with feeling or thought, uplift, etc.) from the technical use of the term to describe the Scriptures.

15. Invite participants to answer the true/false statements. Some may be disputable, but b, c, and j are true; the rest are false. Statements f and g reveal what has been called "Gospel reductionism" or reducing the *inspired* Scriptures merely to the content of the Gospel message. In regard to i, you can point out how most churches do not require women to cover their heads in worship in spite of the clear instructions in 1 Corinthians 11:1–16. However, the principle of "headship" (properly understood) is still relevant. That is the point of statement j.

Read aloud the concluding paragraph of the Focus section.

Divine Author/Human Authors (Inform)

16. Paul is referring specifically to the Old Testament since the New Testament was probably not yet all written and collected in Paul's day. The phrase "God-breathed" in v. 16 has also been translated "inspired." Note that the word for "breath" or "wind" in Greek and Hebrew is the same as the word used for "spirit" and the Holy "Spirit." A connection with the Holy Spirit and inspiration is at least implied. God breathed or God spirited the Scriptures. The use of the word *all* is significant. When used in reference to inspiration, the term *plenary* confesses this truth. Plenary inspiration means everything in the written Scriptures comes "fully" from the breath of God; nothing is excluded.

17. 2 Peter 1 similarly refers to the entire Old Testament at the time Peter is writing. People usually understand prophecy to mean predicting the future. However, the word *prophecy* in the Scriptures is much broader. It means speaking and applying God's will in a variety of different settings. You may point out the following: (1) Moses was the greatest prophet of the Old Testament, (2) in the Hebrew Bible, Moses' writings are followed by the Former Prophets (Joshua through Kings) and then the Latter Prophets (Isaiah, etc.), and (3) the prophets use the majority of their words to speak of the past and present, not simply the future. Prophecy is speaking for God and is God speaking.

Notice again the exclusive terminology ("no prophecy"; "never") for explaining plenary inspiration.

This excludes either the view that the Scriptures are merely a human product (e.g., 15g above) or what is called the "dictation theory" (e.g., 15a above). The latter implies the authors were passive and uninvolved (think of terms like robotic, automatic, mechanical). The origin of Scripture is clearly God, but, at the same time, "men spoke from God." Here you also have a clear reference to the Holy Spirit carrying along those who "spoke from God."

18. By using the phrase "Thus says the LORD" the Old Testament prophets assert that the message they speak is directly from the Lord and spoken in His behalf, as described by the 2 Peter passage above. Their words are the Lord's words! The prophets often spoke of the Word of the Lord coming to them and becoming a part of them. They then "had to" proclaim what the Lord revealed to them.

19. Jeremiah 1:9 declares that the Lord put His words into Jeremiah's mouth. Jeremiah 26:2 is God's command for Jeremiah to speak everything God had revealed to him. Jeremiah 20:9 reveals that even when Jeremiah tried to hold in God's Word, he could not. On the other hand, when Jeremiah received or "ate" the Word of the Lord, this was a great joy according to 15:16. The last passage reveals how the Lord's words became a part of the prophet who "ingested" them. Similar language is used in Ezekiel 2:9–3:4. Notice again how the words to Ezekiel are received, eaten, and then proclaimed. Isaiah's call is similarly "inspiring" (6:1–9). After seeing God on His throne, Isaiah laments his unclean lips. After his mouth is touched with a coal from the altar, he is cleansed from sin. Then Isaiah is able to speak the Word of the Lord.

20a. When Jesus speaks, His words are from the Spirit of God (see 2 Peter 1:20–21 above). They also have the power to give life. Both of these will be dealt with further in the next lesson and "The Word and the Word Made Flesh."

b. Paul speaks of receiving "from the Lord" and "passing on" in these passages. These are technical rabbinic words for accurately and authoritatively receiving words directly or indirectly from the source and then faithfully passing them on just as received. Thus Paul here implies that he is writing the Word of the Lord.

c. The apostle Paul based the authenticity of his Gospel message on the fact that it came by direct revelation from the Lord Jesus.

d. As St. Paul taught in Thessalonica, the believers there did not simply receive the words of Paul. Rather, they comprehended that Paul actually spoke the Word of God to them.

e. In this passage, Paul explicitly asserts that he is writing the Lord's command, not merely his own.

f. 1 Timothy 5:18 quotes Deuteronomy 25:4 and then the words of Jesus recorded in Luke 10:7. Both quotations are introduced with the phrase "For the Scripture says." This reveals that as St. Paul wrote to Timothy, around A.D. 65, Jesus' words were already considered on par with the Old Testament Word of God.

g. In a similar manner, 2 Peter 3:15–16, written about the same time, acknowledges that the writings of St. Paul were being collected, studied, misunderstood, and distorted shortly after they were written! Even more important, the end of verse 16 explicitly groups Paul's writings together with "the other Scriptures." This places his letters on the same level as Jesus' words and the Old Testament.

21. Jesus establishes another link between the Holy Spirit and the Word of the Lord. In John 14 the Holy Spirit teaches the disciples all things and reminds them of everything Jesus said. This explains how we received accurate and reliable written Gospels through the disciples Matthew and John. In addition, Mark's Gospel is traditionally linked with the disciple Peter. Luke also received his information from those "who from the first were eyewitnesses and servants of the word" (Luke 1:2). However, this is not to be limited merely to direct quotations from Jesus in "red-letter" Bibles. It includes all the words of the Lord. In John 16 the Spirit guides people into all truth by hearing from Jesus and then speaking His Word and will to us.

A Great and Holy Helper (Connect)

22. Paul asserts that it is only by receiving the Holy Spirit, who is freely given from God (v. 12), that we are able to understand the spiritual truths of God's spiritual words. Notice that the uses of "spiritual," the references to things that are "spiritually discerned," and the description of a "spiritual" person all are related to the Holy Spirit. In our day, the word *spiritual* tends to have a much broader meaning than in this passage where it is a direct link to the Holy Spirit. The Holy Spirit produced the Scriptures, but His work did not stop there. The Holy Spirit enables people to understand the truths of the

Scriptures and even to know the mind of the Lord Christ (v. 16). The Luke reference notes that Jesus had to open the minds of the first disciples before they could understand that the spiritual truth of the Old Testament is that it foretold the Gospel message.

23. The point is that we should not separate the Spirit from the Word. They come together as "Spirit-filled" words. The passage reasserts the link between Jesus' words, the Holy Spirit who enables us to comprehend them, and the life given by the Spirit through those words.

Every Good Work (Vision)

24. The main task is "to make you wise for salvation through faith in Christ Jesus" (v. 15). However, the God-breathed Scriptures also strive to equip God's people for doing good works (see Ephesians 2:10; 2 Timothy 3:17; the third use of the Law). They do this by identifying which works are good in God's eyes. In addition, by teaching, rebuking, correcting, and training, the Scriptures steer us away from evil and toward good. Yet the Gospel is the primary focus, which provides the proper motivation for what follows.

25. This will be an interesting question for which to hear answers. Any contact we have with the inspired Word of God from the Scripture would qualify, whether it comes by directly reading the Bible, by hearing it read, or as it is utilized by other sources. *Insofar as* a pastor, teacher, book, song, or billboard quotes the Scriptures, those words are inspired since they simply repeat inspired words to begin with. However, this does not make all of a sermon or hymn or song inspired.

God's Pen Is Mightier Than All!

Objectives

By the power of the Holy Spirit working through God's Word, participants will (1) understand that the authority of God's Word is a direct implication of its inspiration, (2) grasp the meaning of the illustrations used in Scripture to describe the power of God's Word, (3) perceive the authority or power of God's Word in terms of both Law and Gospel, and (4) learn how to equip themselves to use the sword of the Spirit, which is the Word of God.

Opening Worship

Sing "Lord, Keep Us Steadfast in Your Word" (*LW* 334), "Almighty God, Your Word Is Cast" (*LW* 342), or "Onward, Christian Soldiers" (*LW* 518). A number of hymns would serve as excellent conclusions to this lesson; however, you may want to use one or two at the beginning and another at the end. Consider using the hymn of Dr. Luther "Lord, Keep Us Steadfast in Your Word" as a sung or spoken prayer. Notice that it uses the sword imagery in a negative manner. Another option is "Almighty God, Your Word Is Cast." It uses the metaphor of a seed which grows and produces new life to describe the Word of God. In view of the Vision at the end of the lesson, one or more stanzas of "Onward, Christian Soldiers" could lead to an inspirational conclusion.

Focus

26. This phrase means that written words are often more powerful than military might. Many times in history the power of words has stood up against and even defeated the power of the sword. The Reformation is clearly one of these cases since the printing press aided in the effort. One could say the writings of Dr. Luther, particularly the Ninety-five Theses, overpowered the strength of the Holy Roman

Emperor. The Declaration of Independence is another example where the strength of words overcame superior military might. See if students come up with other examples.

27. In Ephesians 6:17 St. Paul calls God's Word "the sword of the Spirit." If the sword of the Spirit is God's Word, they are, at least in that analogy, one and the same. The point is that God's Word is the instrument of His Spirit and that it yields considerable power. We will return to this passage in the Vision section.

Power and Authority (Inform)

Point out and, if helpful, discuss the following note: This lesson directly follows ideas from the previous lesson. It is because the Scriptures are the inspired Word of God that they have power and authority.)

28. The Word of the Lord is like rain or snow. Rain and snow come from the skies above and produce fruitful, beneficial results. So it is with the Lord's Word from heaven. It accomplishes the Lord's powerful purpose in sending it.

29. God "said" and created all that exists (e.g., Genesis 1:3).

30. The Lord's Word is like fire and a hammer that breaks rocks to pieces. You could use this to talk about the Law bringing low and breaking down sinful hearts.

31. Instead of being like rain and snow in Isaiah, the Word of God is like a seed in Jesus' parable of the sower. Notice how it can produce amazingly abundant fruit (v. 8). Here the analogy is to the growth and spread of God's kingdom through the ministry of Jesus' Word.

32. This is a very clear statement about the power of God's Word. Discuss the implications of each of these words: *living, active, sharp,* and *penetrating.* It also judges, The imagery of a sword reappears. God's Word cuts through everything else and gets to the heart of the matter!

33. In John 12:48 Jesus says His Word will condemn those who reject both Him and His Word on the Last Day. This is the powerful Law. However, the Greek word for power in Romans 1:16 is *dunamis* from which we get *dynamite* and *dynamic* in English. There Paul stresses that the ultimate power of God is His power to save through the good news of the Gospel. This is an important passage for us to

consider. We usually think of power and authority in terms of the Law. They force, compel, and push down. But, as in the analogies of rain and seed, the power of God's Word is the ultimate *positive* power. It gives life, produces fruit, nourishes, sustains, and saves.

Seeds That Last (Connect)

34. Life apart from God perishes (v. 23). Isaiah 40 is quoted, which speaks of all humans and all human glory as flowers and grass. None of these last; all wither and fade. God's Word, on the other hand, stands forever. Therefore, it powerfully gives imperishable life.

35. These are probably references to Baptism. Point out that the Greek word *baptisma* simply means to wash. We find many references in the Scriptures to Baptism where that specific word is not present (e.g., John 3:3, 5; Ephesians 5:26). According to 1 Peter 1:25, God's Word is proclaimed. But when God's proclaimed Word is combined with water, it produces Christian Baptism. You may want to turn to, read, or review "The Nature of Baptism" and "The Power of Baptism" in Martin Luther's Small Catechism (*Lutheran Worship,* p. 303).

36. The "natural" hunger of a baby is for milk; the "super-natural" hunger of a born-again (1:23) believer is for God's Word. It not only gives imperishable life (v. 23), it also nourishes that life and enables it to grow (2:2). According to 1 Peter 3:21, Baptism, the water and the Word, saves. But the Word then also enables us to grow up in that salvation (2:2). Some see a reference to the Lord's Supper in verse 3 where the Lord's goodness is tasted.

Well-Armed (Vision)

37. The Christian soldier may or may not be a familiar metaphor to the students. If it is not, you may want to describe the equipment of the typical Roman soldier and its purpose. After the verses are read, identify our opponents as the devil's schemes, rulers, authorities and powers of this dark world, and the spiritual forces of evil. We are defended by the armor of truth, righteousness, faith, and salvation. Point out that God stands us up in the faith and equips us so that we are enabled to stay standing (vv. 13–14). "The sword of the Spirit . . . is the word of God" (v. 17).

38. As the Christian reaches out with the sword of the Spirit, the world is often offended by the Law. Its assertion of an overarching, universal morality is offensive to many in our postmodern world. The exclusive claims of the Gospel are also offensive to many in our day who see spiritual truth and legitimacy in almost any and every form of religion (see John 14:6; Acts 4:12). If others are offended by Christianity, it should be God's message of Law and Gospel which offends them, rather than the conduct or abrasiveness of Christians. Verse 15 says we are also equipped with the readiness that comes from the Gospel of peace.

You Have My Word on It!

Objectives

By the power of the Holy Spirit working through God's Word, participants will (1) understand the process by which the Old and New Testament canon came into being, (2) realize the truth claims God's Word makes for itself, (3) grapple with this truth in terms of the apparent paradox of Law and Gospel, (4) identify God's truth with the person of Jesus Christ, and (5) think about other sources of truth in our world and how God's Word relates to them.

Opening Worship

An excellent song for this lesson is "Thy Word" by Michael W. Smith and Amy Grant (*All God's People Sing!* 247). The chorus simply repeats Psalm 119:105. If you are unable to lead it, you may want to bring in a CD or tape of the song and play it.

Focus

Have someone read the first paragraph and discuss it. We all fall short in this area. As a result, this is a good time for self-examination and, perhaps, an opportunity for confession and forgiveness.

Read the rest of the Focus section. This is a little complicated, so you may want to spend some time working through the paragraph of historical review in the Student Guide and answering any questions. Then introduce postmodernism; see if students can identify postmodern trends in education, religion, politics, or other areas.

39. Answers will vary.

One Book, Many Books (Inform)

The issue of the canon is not addressed within the Bible itself and, therefore, is not technically a Bible study topic. However, a short explanation of how the 66 documents in the Scriptures came to be "the Bible" is helpful for this study. Have someone read the three paragraphs provided and respond briefly to any questions. Try to move quickly into the main focus of the lesson.

40a. God's words are flawless and pure, like metal that is perfectly refined.

b. Psalm 119 asserts again and again that the Lord's words, commands, precepts, and laws are true, trustworthy, and eternal. This applies to the Law and its commands, which come from God and do assert an absolute morality of right and wrong. However, the Hebrew word translated "law" (Torah) has a broader meaning ("instruction" or "revelation") which also encompasses the Gospel.

c. God's Word is flawless; His ways are perfect. Notice what follows from this in the Gospel content of the second half of the verse.

d. "Scripture cannot be broken" implies that once God has spoken, His Word stands.

e. Jesus identifies or equates God's Word and truth.

41. This is called the contingency of prophecy. Lutherans have a good insight into these situations with the paradox between God speaking Law and Gospel. The Jeremiah passage spells out in more detail how God is consistent in applying Law or Gospel depending on the circumstances. In Jonah, the Ninevites responded to the proclamation of the Law with repentance, and God relented as He promises in Jeremiah 18. However, Jeremiah also reminds us that those who receive God's grace and then turn away will rightly receive the condemnation of His Law. The marvelous assurance in all this is James 2:13. God's "mercy triumphs over judgment." God's desire to save us through the Gospel is greater than His just determination to punish sinners. Both are true, however.

42. If God's Word is the truth and Jesus is the truth, then it may be proper to equate Jesus with God's Word. This is, in fact, the truth of the next lesson!

True to the Text (Connect)

43. Jesus calls His Father to sanctify Jesus' followers by the truth. The verb "sanctify" means to "make holy" or to "set apart." Notice verse 19 where Jesus hallows or sets Himself apart to accomplish His mission in order that He may make us truly holy (1 Corinthians 1:30).

In verse 17 the point is that God makes us holy; we cannot do it ourselves. Here in John 17:17 this "making us holy" is related directly to the truth which is equated to the Father's Word. As in question 41 above, the primacy of the Gospel is once again stressed. The truth of God's Word is that He desires to make us holy as He is holy. Notice from the Leviticus passage that this was true in the Old Testament. His people were not supposed to try to become holy by keeping the Law; neither were they able to do so. Rather, Leviticus 20:8 states that the Lord made them holy or sanctified them just as Jesus says in John 17:17! Leviticus 11:45 points out that the people's motivation for trying to live holy lives was a response to the Gospel of the exodus and a desire to be like the God who had already saved them and made them holy.

44. The tendency of the Pharisees and the teachers of the law was to equate their oral traditions with the Word of God. In Matthew 15:6 Jesus condemns them for setting aside or even nullifying the Word of God for the sake of their tradition. Throughout its history, the church has also exhibited a tendency to elevate tradition to the level of God's Word or even higher. This creates disharmony among the church's members and confuses the unbelieving world. Martin Luther fought the traditions of papal power by asserting "Scripture alone" as the sole source of authority in the church. We must be careful to speak with the authority of God's Word where God's Word speaks but also make clear when that is not the case.

Certain Truth (Vision)

45. People will probably identify the creation account (Genesis 1–2), Noah's ark and the flood (Genesis 6–9), the sun standing still in Joshua 10, and the miracles present in Jesus' ministry and throughout the Scriptures. The Christian may respond that such events are supernatural since God's intervention is directly involved. As a result, those events are logically contrary to the normal workings of nature and its laws. While it is impossible to prove such events, it is also impossible to disprove them. If God and the supernatural are excluded at the outset, some other explanation must be made (e.g., naturalistic evolution, the early church made up the miracles, etc.). A Christian's response will vary according to the circumstances. However, the Christian faith is just that, a faith. "Faith is being sure of what we hope

for and certain of what we do not see. . . . By faith we understand that the universe was formed at God's command" (Hebrews 11:1, 3).

46. The conviction that the Scriptures are true or inerrant is properly a conviction of faith, as noted at the end of the previous answer. Any society with no absolute truths is headed toward chaos. Civilization must have some overarching, moral truths. Even if these are not directly from or based upon Scripture, they can make decent order in a society (see Romans 2:12–16). This recognizes that there are other human sources of truth. For example, we have learned much about ourselves and the world around us through the fields of psychology, biology, anthropology, and so forth. Many of the "truths" discovered in these areas have supplemented the truths of the Scriptures, rather than competing against them. But the Scriptures do not simply assert themselves to be one truth among many other truths. They claim to be *the* truth with a capital *T*. They reveal the truth about the one true God and His relationship with humanity.

The Word and
the Word Made Flesh

Objectives

By the power of the Holy Spirit working through God's Word, participants will (1) realize that the fulfillment of the Old Testament is found in the person and work of Jesus Christ, who is the center and focus of the entire Scriptures, (2) comprehend that the eternal Word of God was made flesh in the person of Jesus Christ (the incarnation), (3) grasp the truth that the Word of God stands forever, and (4) strive to continue to "grow in the grace and knowledge of our Lord and Savior Jesus Christ. To Him be glory both now and forever! Amen" (2 Peter 3:18).

Opening Worship

"O Word of God Incarnate" (*LW* 335) has a number of good links with this concluding lesson. It explicitly identifies Jesus as the Word made flesh (v. 1). In addition, the Word of God is the treasured gift received by the church (v. 2) but one that is also to shine "before the nations" (v. 3).

Focus

Before reading the introductory paragraphs, ask the students to state some of the significant things they have learned in this study. You may use questions like "What sticks out in your mind from the last four lessons?" and "What will you remember most from this study so far?" Then have someone read the paragraphs.

Getting to the Point (Inform)

47a. The Old Testament Scriptures testify to Jesus. Note that Jesus does not contradict their conclusion that, at the same time, the Scriptures also point the way to eternal life.

b. Jesus asserts that Moses "wrote about Me!" Believing in Moses (i.e., Genesis through Deuteronomy) would mean believing in Jesus as well. What does this say about the Jewish people today? See Acts 4:23–26.

c. Everything the Old Testament said about the coming Messiah, or Christ, has been fulfilled in the suffering, death, and resurrection of Jesus. Jesus opened their minds so they could see He was the fulfillment of it all.

48. Hebrews begins by asserting that Jesus, God's Son, is the final and ultimate way in which God has spoken to His people. 1 Peter 1:10–12 suggests that the Old Testament writers wrote about and eagerly anticipated the salvation which has now come through the suffering and glory of Christ. While they did not fathom the exact when or how of the fulfillment, the Spirit of Christ was, nevertheless, pointing them ahead to Jesus.

49. Jesus declares that His own words, in conjunction with the Word of God in the Old Testament (Deuteronomy 8:3), are Spirit and Life. Peter affirms that Jesus speaks words of "eternal life."

50. "God said" (Genesis 1:3, etc.). All that exists came into being by God speaking His Word.

51. The Word was in the beginning with God and, in fact, the Word was God (1:1). All things were created through that Word (1:3). John 1:14 is the incarnation in its most straightforward language. The Word became flesh in Jesus, the babe, the Son of Mary. The Word was God (John 1:1), and the Word-God became human flesh (1:14). That is the joyful message of Jesus' conception and birth that was revealed in a dream to Joseph (Matthew 1:20–21) and to the Virgin Mary by the angel Gabriel (Luke 1:35).

52. John again identifies Jesus as the Word of Life who was from all eternity. In Jesus, the Word became flesh, a physical human being. As John and the other disciples heard, saw, looked at, and touched the human body of Jesus, they encountered "the Word of life" in the flesh. The purpose of the incarnation was to bring us into fellowship with the Father through the Son, and ultimately with each other (v. 3). Sharing

this message so that others have fellowship with us makes our joy complete (v. 4).

53. The same author who wrote the Gospel and 1 John again pictures Jesus for us, but this time in the apocalyptic imagery of Revelation. Jesus is called "Faithful and True" (v. 11; see also John 14:6). He judges and makes war (v. 11). He is dressed in a robe dipped in blood (v. 13). He has a sword coming from His mouth (v. 15; see also 1:16; Ephesians 6:13). On His robe and thigh is written the name "KING OF KINGS AND LORD OF LORDS" (v. 16; see "The Hallelujah Chorus" of Handel's *Messiah*). The end of verse 13 specifically identifies *His name* as "the Word of God" (see also John 1:1, 14).

Finding the Center (Connect)

54. As New Testament Christians, we often neglect the Old Testament in our devotions, our discussions, and our worship. Instead, we should eagerly "study the Scriptures" (John 5:39) and "the whole will of God" (Acts 20:27).

55. We now read the Old Testament through the events of the birth, life, ministry, death, resurrection, ascension, reign, and promised return of Jesus Christ. We view those Scriptures as fulfilled in Christ but also can see more in the Old Testament now that the bud of God's plan of salvation has fully flowered (see 1 Peter 1:10–12 above). For example, one can perceive the three persons of the Trinity at work in Genesis 1:1–3. The Father created (v. 1); the Son was the Word (v. 3); the Spirit was hovering (v. 2). Hosea 11:1 can simply be a statement about the exodus of God's people from Egypt, but now, in the fullness of time, it is more completely embodied in Jesus' return from Egypt in Matthew 2:14–15, 19–21. God's Old Testament people came out of Egypt, through the waters of the Red Sea, and out into the wilderness for 40 years. In Matthew's Gospel, Jesus comes out of Egypt, through the waters of His baptism, and out into the wilderness for 40 days (Matthew 2, 3, and 4). Psalm 22:1 is David's desperate cry when he felt forsaken by God; it is fully and absolutely experienced by Jesus on the cross (Mark 15:34). Many further examples could be cited.

56. Jesus assures us that when the world as we know it comes to an end, He is coming to take us home, our redemption is drawing near (Luke 21:28). If all else fails and falls apart, including the heavens and earth as we know them, His Word will never pass away (Luke 21:33).

At the conclusion of this section, reread the following passage from 1 Peter which quotes Isaiah 40: "'The grass withers and the flowers fall, but the word of the Lord stands forever.' And this is the word that was preached to you" (1 Peter 1:24b–25). This leads directly into the closing Vision.

Growing in the Gift (Vision)

57. A baby is born alive and is no more or less alive as he or she grows up from infancy through adulthood. In a similar manner, we are born again in Baptism through the power of God's enduring Word (1 Peter 1:23; 3:21). We are alive in relationship with God and cannot become any "more" alive. But, just as a child grows, so we can grow up in our knowledge and our living out of the salvation God has bestowed upon us.

58. You may want to allow participants silent time to write down a resolution to continue growing in God's Word. Some examples you could suggest are these: start a new Bible class; join an existing Bible class; read through the Bible in a year; listen to the Bible regularly on tape or CD. Make sure they understand this is not a legalistic exercise but a response to tasting the goodness of God's Word and simply wanting more! This desire or craving is motivated by God's Spirit and strives to allow God to draw us ever closer to Him as we are exposed to His holy and precious Word.

A closing prayer or time of sharing may be appropriate. You may read the words of "God's Word Is Our Great Heritage" (*LW* 333) as a conclusion to the study. They are printed in the group lesson. This text works with the tune of "A Mighty Fortress" (*LW* 297), but you should probably practice it first!

Appendix of Lutheran Teaching

Below you will find examples of how the first Lutherans described God's Word. They will help you understand the Lutheran difference.

The Augsburg Confession of 1530

Philip Melanchthon, a lay associate of Dr. Martin Luther, wrote the Augsburg Confession to clarify for Emperor Charles V just what Lutherans believed. Melanchthon summarized Lutheran teaching from the Bible and addressed the controversies of the day. This confession remains a standard of Lutheran teaching.

Conclusion

Only those things have been recounted whereof we thought that it was necessary to speak, in order that it might be understood that in doctrine and ceremonies nothing has been received on our part against Scripture or the Church Catholic. For it is manifest that we have taken most diligent care that no new and ungodly doctrine should creep into our churches (*Concordia Triglotta*, p. 95).

Apology of the Augsburg Confession

Philip Melanchthon also wrote the Apology to further explain Lutheran beliefs.

Article IV 5

All Scripture ought to be distributed into these two principal topics, the Law and the promises. For in some places it presents the Law, and in others the promise concerning Christ, namely, either when it promises Christ will come, and offers, for His sake, the remission of sins, justification, and life eternal, or when, in the Gospel, Christ Himself, since He has appeared, promises the remission of sins, justification, and life eternal (*Concordia Triglotta*, p. 121).

Small Catechism

Luther wrote his Small Catechism, or little manual for Christian instruction, in 1528. His intention was to give heads of households, normally fathers, a booklet for teaching the basics of the Christian faith to all those under their care. Both Luther's Small and Large Catechisms were first published in 1529 and have been used by the Lutheran church in the instruction of youth and adults for nearly 500 years.

Part I: The Third Commandment, 5–6

Thou shalt sanctify the holy-day. *What does this mean?*

We should fear and love God that we may not despise preaching and His Word, but hold it sacred, and gladly hear and learn it. (See also The Large Catechism, The Ten Commandments, 91–93, C*oncordia Triglotta*, p. 607.)

Part III: The Lord's Prayer: The First Petition, 3–5

Hallowed be Thy name. *What does this mean?*

God's name is indeed holy in itself; but we pray in this petition that it may become holy among us also.

How is this done?

When the Word of God is taught in its truth and purity, and we as the children of God also lead holy lives in accordance with it. To this end help us, dear Father in heaven. But he that teaches and lives otherwise than God's Word teaches profanes the name of God among us. From this preserve us, Heavenly Father. (See also The Second and Third Petitions, 6–11, *Concordia Triglotta*, p. 547, and The Sacrament of the Altar, 76, p. 771.)

Formula of Concord

Following Luther's death in 1546, confusion disrupted the Lutheran churches. Some wished to compromise on matters of doctrine in order to attain greater peace and unity with Calvinists and Roman Catholics. Others claimed to be true Lutherans but strayed from Luther's teaching. In 1576 Elector August of Saxony called a conference to clarify the issues. The result was the Formula of Concord (*concord* means "unity"), published in 1580.

Epitome Summary, 1

We believe, teach, and confess that the sole rule and standard according to which all dogmas together with teachers should be estimated and judged are the prophetic and apostolic Scriptures of the Old and of the New Testament alone, as it is written (Psalm 119:105): *Thy Word is a lamp unto my feet and a light unto my path.* And St. Paul: *Though an angel from heaven preach any other gospel unto you, let him be accursed* (Galatians 1:8) (*Concordia Triglotta,* p. 777).

Epitome Summary, 7

In this way the distinction between the Holy Scriptures of the Old and of the New Testament and all other writings is preserved, and the Holy Scriptures alone remain the only judge, rule, and standard, according to which, as the only test-stone, all dogmas shall and must be discerned and judged, as to whether they are good or evil, right or wrong (*Concordia Triglotta,* p. 779).

Solid Declaration Summary, 3

1. First, then, we receive and embrace with our whole heart *the Prophetic and Apostolic Scriptures of the Old and New Testaments* as the pure, clear fountain of Israel, which is the only true standard by which all teachers and doctrines are to be judged (*Concordia Triglotta,* p. 851).

Solid Declaration XI 12

To this false delusion and thought we should oppose the following clear argument, which is sure and cannot fail, namely . . . all Scripture, given by inspiration of God, is to serve, not for security and impenitence, but *for reproof, for correction, for instruction in righteousness,* 2 Timothy 3:16; also . . . everything in God's Word has been prescribed to us, not that we should thereby be driven to despair, but *that we, through patience and comfort of the Scriptures, might have hope,* Romans 15:4 (*Concordia Triglotta,* p. 1067).

Glossary

antinomianism. The belief that Christians are free from many, if not all, of the constraints of moral law.

Apocrypha. A collection of noncanonical books written during the intertestamental period. Luther's Bible of 1534 included the Apocrypha between the Old and New Testaments with this remark: "Apocrypha: These books are not held equal to the Sacred Scriptures, and yet are useful and good for reading."

canon. A Greek word meaning "rule" or "list," and when used of the Scriptures indicates those books having authority and inspiration as the Word of God. Lutherans affirm the canon of the 66 books of the Old and New Testaments. The canon was determined by the church because the individual books and letters agreed with prophetic and apostolic teaching.

evangelical. Literally, "good news"—the Gospel. This term is often used to describe churches that stress the Gospel of Jesus Christ in their teachings, especially His death and resurrection to save people from their sin and grant them eternal life.

filioque. Literally, "and the Son." This phrase was added to the Nicene Creed in the West to emphasize that the Holy Spirit proceeds from the Father *and the Son.*

fundamentalism. A reactionary movement against liberalism and modernism that focuses on certain cardinal tenets of the Christian faith—biblical inerrancy among them—often to the exclusion of other beliefs. Liberal Christians often accuse those believing in biblical inerrancy of being "fundamentalists."

Gospel. The message of Christ's death and resurrection for the forgiveness of sins and eternal life. The Holy Spirit works through the Gospel to create and sustain faith, and to empower good works. The Gospel is found in both the Old and New Testaments.

Gospel reductionism. Using the Gospel to suggest considerable latitude in faith and life in ways not explicitly detailed in the Gospel. Associated with liberal Christianity, Gospel reductionism is closely aligned with **antinomianism** and **partial inspiration** (see definition to *partial inspiration* on p. 21).

holy. Set apart for a divine purpose (e.g., Holy Scripture is set apart from all other types of writing). The Holy Spirit makes Christians holy (see **sanctification**).

inerrancy. The teaching that the Bible, as originally inspired by the Holy Spirit and recorded by the prophets, apostles, and evangelists, did not contain errors. Churches teaching biblical inerrancy recognize that scribes and translators may have erred in copying the Bible over the centuries.

inspiration. Guidance by a spirit. In many religions the term describes a trancelike state of spirit possession. In Christianity the term usually describes the guidance of God's Holy Spirit provided to the prophets and the writers of the Bible (plenary or verbal inspiration).

justification. God declares sinners to be just or righteous for Christ's sake; that is, God has imputed or charged our sins to Christ and He imputes or credits Christ's righteousness to us.

Law. God's will which shows people how they should live (e.g., the Ten Commandments) and condemns their failure. The preaching of the Law is the cause of contrition, or genuine sorrow over sin. The Law is found in both the Old and New Testaments.

polemical. From the Greek word for "battle." The term describes conversation or writing that attacks and refutes.

sanctification. The spiritual growth that follows justification by grace through faith in Christ.